Other Books by Laura Jensen

AFTER I HAVE VOTED (1972)

ANXIETY AND ASHES (1976)

BAD BOATS (1977)

TAPWATER (1978)

THE STORY MAKES THEM WHOLE (1979)

Memory

MEMORY

by

Laura Jensen

Dragon Gate, Inc.

Poems in this collection were first published in the following periodicals: AMERICAN POETRY REVIEW, ANDOVER REVIEW, ANTAEUS, ARTREACH, CHOWDER REVIEW, CRAZYHORSE, FIELD, GILTEDGE, IOWA REVIEW, IRONWOOD, MONTANA REVIEW, PIERCE COUNTY POETRY 1975, POETRY NORTHWEST and RACCOON. "Memory," "Kite" and "The Kiss" were first published in THE NEW YORKER. Some poems were published in *Tapwater* (Graywolf Press, 1978). Two poems have been published as broadsides by Sea Pen Press.

The author would like to thank the Washington State Arts Commission for their Honors Award in Poetry, 1978-79, and the National Endowment for the Arts for their Fellowship Grant, 1980-81.

Library of Congress #81-67640
ISBN 0-937872-02-4
    0-937872-03-2 (paper)

First printing, 1982

Published by DRAGON GATE, INC., 508 Lincoln St., Port Townsend, Washington 98368.

Contents

Memory

The falcon is directed by an arm,
flies into the sky and does not return.
The falconer stands astonished,
dangling the leather hood. A little
wine, some mild laughing, and the king
forgets, but the falconer lies in bed
staring at the ceiling or the plate
of stars at the bare window.

Then in the dark there is a sound,
and the bird has returned to him,
knowing the way by night, flying in
to the falconer's chamber. Proud
as a cat it drops the prey: a debt.
It looks at the man with one eye,
speaks in one of the falcon
dialects, unable to express
where it has been as it toured the sky.
Did it follow above the lake,
the village, forest and mountain?
Does it recall?

By night a forgotten name
will rise to the unfortunate
who stood there silent and foolish
by day. The falcon knows the falconer
with both its eyes. Like memory, it
returned when it was unexpected.
Like memory it is a weight on the arm,
missed sorely when it is missing.

I

Mouse

Mother picked up the fantastic cup,
washed the idea of dishes, hovered over
the stove-notion behind a make-believe curtain.
Saw her children not-wake, go away asleep
wearing coats like their blankets. And not aware
of much but the tender feel at the edge
of the evergreen, the pout of the fattening berry.

Eyes spending butter on a clock
cannot make their own way up to midnight, up to noon,
or to the falling
crying mamma, mamma,
I do not want to go on.
There's a song from the bottle,
from the seashell, from the sharp beak
of the seagull: *pain be gone.*

Autumn, and the pear skin does not want to curl.

Mother pear, mother pearl, can you follow
what I am telling? Mother, the idea of love
wraps around us like a quilt of old morning,
like a horseshoe of flowers.

Ah, they are small, small, sleep in the stomach.
Ah, they are small, small, little rodents of love.

Somali Legend

A couple carrying too many
water jars could not carry
their baby. They left him safely
where they could find him—
underneath the moon.
    —a story from NEW WIND IN A DRY LAND
        by Margaret Laurence

Where the shallow spring sings in the night,
ripples white in the moon's reflection,
mother, oh mother,
you dip our water jars.
Mother, mother,
I have not left your pale milk yet.
Why do you trust the glitter
that brought you agony,
that brought you me?
You are leaving my small cries to the moon,
it shrinks and fattens up again on me,
here where the night sand is cold.
Mother, mother!
Never again will I see you. I know this
as you walk away toward heaven.

One day I might be at the village,
hear of my mother at the gate:
that she could not bear to look at the moon.
That one day she looked at blue sky,
that then she fell dead as though the point
of the early crescent pierced her heart.
That the goats of the village
are born blind in one eye.
That their good eye shines white-yellow,
ever since she could not take me with her.

Hot Gravel

Hot gravel we walked on,
gravel pressing into the callus
that starts in the womb, pressing
and never piercing,
never blood but smooth dark dirt.
How the dark was light
indoors, windows darker
with the white porcelain
ungiving to the small squashed calves
like sail on bone. So bright,
white shallow water cleans
your feet again, mother,
my heart breaks when I share
my feet with anyone else.
Oh, my heart breaks
just to share them.
Your child kneels again
at the window, the dark
is cool and a beacon
blinks on the radio tower.
Light pajamas, thin cotton
and everything
is clean, or dark, or cool
and blinking on and on,
forever let me hear
the drawer close, keep me
kneeling there a while,
let me hear the drawer close
as I sleep clustered
like your one bud of the night.
Let me hear the drawer
close in the old soft cabinet,
the rolling wood on wood
to conclusion.

The Creature
from the Black Lagoon

The woman is swimming. Her suit
has molded cups and a flap
of fabric veiling the crotch.
She is unafraid, she is swimming
and beneath her swims
the Creature. He follows
like a shadow and looks up
at her as she crosses the surface,
as she crosses his mirror of sun.

I remember him
haul himself out of the water,
swaying as he stepped
out of his dream
and I stood up in the loge
of the Proctor Theater,
and that night had hysterics
expecting him to expand
the crack at the door of the closet.
I was five, and slept
upstairs, and my sister
could not stop me,
could not make me stop wailing.

Mother,
why did you bring me,
a little girl,
to see the Creature
New Year's Day
1954
or 1953?

For years I would stare
at the door of the closet
and be afraid to turn away.
I grew tired of sleeping
on that same bent side.
And even now
I cannot turn from creaks
in the floor,
from cracks
in the table.
I keep my eyes open and have to see
if something is terribly wrong here.

World War Two Movie:
Home Front

Must it be so public, so private?
Her furniture stalks up and down the stair,
one chair on the landing. Smoke wails out
of the chimney. And many frames before,
the marching military band of comfort,
this actress an American Beauty rose.
That is past tense, time passed at the show—
the year in undecoded Roman numerals—
where it is the wires, the yellow papers
taking their toll. Just when the place
has come to be peaceful, there's a sound
outside the door, and it's Death rapping.
But if Death can rap, there is a place outside
that door, where we can enter, we can say
Do not let us see you weeping anymore.

Living at Home

I saw sad things.
I saw the legs of a dog
crumble under him.
I saw a boy on cloud street
reach above his head
for the W A L K button.
I saw him carry his satchel.
God help him, he was
walking to the office.
If he can carry that satchel
through cloud street
through childhood
and find delight in nothing,
maybe when he's got away
wings of his joy will come out.
The tired clerical garments
will lift themselves out
of his satchel, he will give them
to a man who is weary of joy,
he will find himself on walls,
on the chipping blue paint
of some town like a dumpling,
he will eat the blue paint,
he will taste the sidewalk,
and make the living he made
those years on cloud street.

Kite

Dime store. The goldfish swam in the murky
back. I was a child there, where the helmeted
diver bubbled, where, in an enameled
white basin below, the turtles struggled.
They were a moist delight.
And, as I realize,
shaped as a child draws any animal:
round body, legs and head extending.

Kites are separate from toys, for they are
Seasonal. Toys are in the inner aisles
that follow age so faithfully a child
might guess what the next step might be.
Of skeins of baby yarn, of bibs and rattles
sings the hardwood floor—of mother. Then
of pencils, parties, powder, bobby pins, barrettes.
Suddenly, at the counter, a life has passed—
a history, an age, a generation.

But the kites, like the pleated paper bells,
are Seasonal. Making conversation,
the young father tells, "We're not looking
for some expensive kite now," as his son
and little daughters skip around grandly.

For months it was
Wouldn't your mother like a handkerchief
or perhaps a teapot for Christmas?
in the window display,
but now it is kites and flowers.

Not kites in trees or kites like heroines
in wires, but the kite that was a speck,
the opposite of fishing: to want nothing
caught in anything but the pretty sky,
to reel the color back down again
beside you, a celebrity who tells
what it is like in the altitude.

The Seaside Promenade:
Oregon, the Early 60's

Thirsty for salt, the expedition
boiled part of the Pacific Ocean
in a kettle here. Lewis and Clark
might have squatted before the fire,
sipping the brew like chefs, while
Sacajawea faced the ocean,
filling her moccasins with sand.

Imagine salt, necessary, primitive,
holding Europe together. Or imagine
your mother, boiling the year's supply,
white turret-towers of jars
regimental in the cellar.

My sister was steering the tandem
bicycle; I was behind. Quarreling,
we journeyed the length of the Promenade.
Gray weather caught us at the end
where the chain slipped off a wheel.
A little overbearing, cross with me,
she set it straight before our hour was gone.

The next thing I remember, we were
feeding gulls, avoiding their huge, close
bodies, listening to their wings.

The young crowded onto the main street
in the summer night. We walked up and down,
eating breaded hot dogs on a stick,
passing motorcycles, big dogs on chains,
gangs swaggering under artificial light.
They ignored the ocean. At night

it is blank, the sand is gray
or black, and from the Promenade

you hear the shouts—
gangs getting ready for the riot.
Labor Day, back home,
we see them on television,
boys bent by hurrying police,
caught in a floodlight on the night sand.

Salt can be bought by the truckload,
as can sand, speeding hysterically
on the highway away from a refinery.
It melts into our selves like snow.

Out of the curdling mass of young, maybe
some will survive to stand at eighty
alone on a shriveling promenade,
able to see, to hear.

Lipstick

Cosmetics are your noble
benefactors, far away
at department stores,
where the counter girls
glare at your pale face,
thinking you shoplift.
You try a perfume and carry it
at your now-royal wrist
through all the rest.

The store
is crowded and terrible. The lips
of the women are red like alleys
of cardinals, eyes are green
like alleys of bamboo. But none
of the colognes are like the scent of snow
on bamboo, or rutted snow
by the trees where cardinals slum
alertly, saying, *Light. Morning.*

In the alley of *now* the dusk is
trying out the garbage cans. Among them
I am looking around at the dark
after squashing down the trash somehow.
Suspended in the heavens of
the third floor, steam is still blurring
my mirror, soap still haunting the air.
My lipstick clings, cosmetic,
reassuring, its scent feminine and hearty.

Dream: I am an Oriental print.
I turned to walk down the road
after companions when suddenly my face
stopped living, a window painted shut.
Of me there were single hairs, brown with damp.
I was looking up. In the white air by me
there was printed an emblem in a black square,
a signature. I was what was there.

The Teller of Fortunes

The Eye of God swung back
and forth, it dangled
from the mirror. There were
board homes of white and green,
there was the narrow sidewalk
but her eye was on the Eye of God
and it swung before
the department store. When the car
stopped moving it stopped
swinging.
She followed the Eye of God
in her mind's eye.

A dog trotted by. Two girls.
And the Midwestern wife
held out a palm
that had been known to hold
a lifetime.

I see a river.
There is a child watching geese.
It is not in this country.

No. That is my past.
I want to know the future.

Give me your palm.
I see a storm.
I see laundry on a line.
A fat man in a black suit
is coming for the laundry
from a metal garage. He wears
a clerical collar.
I see you!
You take the clothespins
from his hands. You take
the towels.
You will go on a long journey.

II

The Goodyear Blimp

The Goodyear Blimp has lost itself,
has gone down peaceful in a cornfield.
The grounded pilot walks out of the field,
no one hurt, no one around but the blackbirds,
who laughed and kept laughing. He walked
down the empty road in the middle of the day.
It was fine to be uninjured,
to have hurt no one, to walk
in the brief sweet world of the saved.

Hot Spell

Listen to the mower with the shallow blade,
flooding its catcher with a green river.
Listen to the knives and cups. Children
are hooting down in the morning. Take them
whole, like medicine, like loaves of bread.
At the baker's an apron fits around the good,
pocket handy as a thumb. The train whistles
in the distance. Heart, I can hear you
falling, rising, pasty and full. I look up
as it is life to do. Do not look up too often.
Tempers shorten. There are flat, solemn shingles
stained leafy with shadow on the wall. The sun
hangs there like frost.

The light and the tree are twins, two wings
that shelter the avenue. Deep and heavy
spread the golden roots, puffy and gnarled.
From the ground the roses crawl the wall
like savages, in their own kind of logic
and catharsis. Meanwhile, birds dip into
the air. Like metal talismans,
telephone numbers, birds can remember
the nests. The sky hangs like wash.
The people are tired, call sleep that shallow
miser, adjourning and standing on a cloud.
Open their mouths and let sparrows abide there.

Under the Trees

Suddenly the park is quiet,
she has a blade of grass to look for
silently. The attention, the lawn's
attention, grows up at her like rising
pinnacles to the quality of the sky.
Under the leaves of trees, by their rumpled
bark, she wraps the crusts. He stands,
picks the watermelon up, and tosses it—
it falls back down into his hands. She does
not see this, she does not notice at all.

A Confessional Poem
about Two Finches

Small things. I was spending money.
The clerk wrapped up the cage in paper.
I brought it on the bus
to a complicated girl, whose hair
was brushed in a frenzy.
To keep a light alive requires
much brushing, much sun.
She was lonely, her job
would send her back slowly. The shoes
she left in the hallway were proud shoes,
shoes that would not keep finches
anywhere but in the sun.

The birds belonged to me. The pain
and the trap they were caught in, the sun
that would not let them be, the world
that became for them a light
of a bad intensity was mine.
Oh, I gave them only away, and the sad
bodies, brown and red, feathered
like clouds, like leaves lay solid.

They are gone. Sunlight comes back,
wind-music, and music
that begins about four during the summer.
I have no idea where that girl
is living, but I believe she lives.
And I believe the death of the finches
did not radiate from us, but from the death
around us in the beautiful light.

The Cutting Back

As I have been here, the summer has come to be
long ago, and the summer before,
when the chain saws made the trees pale
monoliths, longer ago. I run past—
running must be like confessional,
the same sins, the same houses,
the next day the same sins again—
the two trees, pollarded, reaching
from the ground like gnarled, drowning hands.

The cutting back
has always read to me *slaughter*, even
a man I met; he was whistling, taking
clippers to a hedge—but maybe
it relieves this tree and its fabled
roots—the big, supporting root,
the young, thrusting one.

All there is to do is to wait. The sin
will seem untroubling, the scars
melt into landscape, the trees
assimilate the wrong. In their
sacrificial heart you will wait so long
you will believe this.

To a Stranger (at the End
of a Caboose)

There is a sway that comes soon after
a question. Oatheart, riding a train
in another language, turns from tense
to tense around a verb wheel, its maze
and answer like an angel that missed Adam
and followed like a leaf into traffic.

Summer was a boxcar, never abandoned,
never reclaimed. Summer was unsteady
in detail. He had coveted the thistles
from Rock Island to the Reading,
and seen from a train vitality;
there's more to a farm than patience.

But here are the children side by side
apart from the arty barren farmhouse, really
traveling with the weight of the stack
of their pumpkins, each hauled from the vine
like a suitcase or a sack of money.

In the inner wheel of Oatheart's head
they are traveling farther than the road
from the world in their winter backdrop;
traveling themselves, why not? Changed
by the train wheel, and by afterthoughts.

Starlings

Outside the window, at the top
of a chimney, two starlings are bathing
in soot. In a flock they grind away
at the grass, fly away like wagons
with sticking wheels. How they make
their presumptuous wishes,
what they practice in solitude,
must be therapy, concord, and sleep.
They hang there in some indifferent
tree, dream their boring dreams
which they consider luminary.

They have always just-sprung from some horn
of plenty, they hop like rabbits,
like a gang of kids. As they pound
up to the trees they are like a veil
trailing, a veil you pray beneath.
They are like prayers for the lifting
of that veil. They are not beautiful.

It is cold. I lean at the radiator.
In one of my panes of glass, a man fills
his birdbath, the stream of water glitters
all this way to the other side of the street.
They might bathe, they might bathe forever
and be yet speckled, gritty, holy only
by name. They bear their stars
crudely, yet believe me, they are Earth's
creatures; suet and seed are cool and good.

Last Saturday of the Year

At the landing is a sense of propriety.
I cannot name the cluster of birds
that rock on the waves. They have long necks
with white stripes to the breast.

I must see the *Vashon* with my own eyes.
Soon she is leaving these waters.
Certainly in love, certainly in the coming
decade, certainly on the ferry you never
know whether you are coming or going.
I must see the *Vashon* with my own eyes.

Long enough to stand and remember
Anne Sexton dangling her car keys
on the other side of the nation, long enough
to watch a trailer of horses loaded,
a pink-cheeked girl with tickets
pick up her money box and board.
Then the wake, and little ghosts of oil
around pilings.

At the other side is another bird
I cannot name, a bird
with broad wings he folds
after circling. He bows down enormous
the green branch of the madrona tree.

And it is noon. A cock crows.
Christ.
It is like a thin wolf crying.
I lean over, look back past the body
of the ferry at the smokestack on pink sky.

And before I go home from the *Vashon*
which is leaving these waters which are
so massed with life, so crowded with
the old and new that the passage in or out
of anywhere is a trip through a maze,
I stop for coffee.
The chair seat is beautiful. It is round
with a pattern of water lilies, cattails,
flags, pale brown on a brown ground.

January Visit

Friday morning on the beach
you stalked back up the tracks
to find your leather gloves.
I thought you had left me
by the train-sized FLAMMABLE drums
down the rails from the mill.
We had come a fair way between the sound
of rocks tumbling under waves
and the green weeds frozen
in clear pools, in silence
my bent stick could not shatter.
Everywhere, there was hoarfrost.

The last thing you would do
would be to give me something
I could write about. So I dropped
my magazine into the bus seat
and looked for my last sight of you,
smiling, holding up your rock.
You had picked it up on the cold beach
Friday morning, dark gray
with a white ring, and I assume
the white passes through the rock
clean, unblemished, unblemishing,
and signifies a good thing.

III

Poem

Sleep kept snowing down while she was talking,
and when she left I slept. The snow came,
boxing the houses like jewelry in cotton.

I look down at the street, chewing biscuits.
I nearly asked her to guess about the sapling,
what it truly was: something with a root
to worry over, bendable and alone.

There are white goats in the alleys, bushes
honey-white in the grass-preserve,
there are drooling clappers inside bells,
fundamental diaphanous memories.

From autumn on, eat nothing shaped like a heart.
What is once is again, the clear sky peals.
So I ride uphill, as the sun is setting.
So I ride uphill, as the winter is less severe.

The Moon Rises

The moon rises,
a queen on horseback
exiting a crowded wood.
You pick at your face and mumble,
tired of standing.
Couples hang together,
dance four-legged like a horse.
Sometimes they falter,
fall on knees and hands,
burying their faces in grass.
Next comes the snow you dreamed of:
paper-thin wide wafers
with the glitter of sugar, large,
large, glassy patterns,
and the money, half-dollars
filling the pockets of your robe.
You dream of finding Hemingway's
Lost Suitcase, high in a closet
at the top of a secondary schoolhouse,
and your bicycle, useless
as the hen that towed it,
dead as a stone.
In the grass your feet and bottom
prickle numb.
You carry yourself
home in a wagon
like a farmer's sack.
Whether empty or full
you look back. Just lifting
your glittering eyes above the tailgate
you see the dreamers, still dancing,
fallen like stone.

I Am Your Stone

suggested by a poem by Brian Topping

The stones refuse to touch each other.
They wear hard suits with metal buttons.
They are dark as cake in the middle.
Devil's food cake.
                    The devil farmer
grew them from seeds of stone into knives
and lightning, wheeled his whetstone
into the field.
                    They are never in bloom,
or in season, or in style. They are
inedible. Swallow a stone and the whole
day will go wrong for you; imaginary
aspirin, they will make you choke.

Choose one and it will spring into
your hand so easily, crying Ah ha!
Stones are! But the wind will come back
for them: What did you do with my kisses
of stone? Where are the pearls that hailed
from the sky?
                    The earth is their old
friend. They look in as into a mirror,
through as through a pane of glass, and draw
their own conclusion.
                    They are common
as hearts, and crack almost as easily.

A good stone will do nothing while you
watch it. Tie on some strings, and they
are balloons. I am your stone. But do
not expect me to float in the sky above you.

Tapwater

You live where the sounds of trucks
come through the open window,
packers bringing carcasses at night.
All this time on the side of the market
hang, like eclipses, six round lamps.

But once you went into song, went
into dance, when the rock of night
was lifted, before you thought of all
the things a rock could do to you,
on its own.

Out on the beach the mussels caught
at it, what you overturned;
the crabs scattered, running
with one glance
at some horrible maturity.

You pray to the bird in your hands
that you will never wake again
to that dilemma, or wake without
breath, or without the familiar
town, or without the others.

West Window

The rows of plants send out tentative answers
and some of them are wrong, perhaps, but
the sun is their teacher, not I. They stand
as if for a photograph in their separate pots,
dependent but confiding in no one.

The room of a person, that china teacup
of civilized snow, makes the way of a thing
take light, was here yesterday and every day
changes. The new leaf hesitates but is not lost,
and it is not vanity to be a woman

who is no more than tenant, daughter,
follower, fan, vine, parade, and borrower.

In the span of a month I have touched a horse,
drawn a woman in a girdle of half-moons
and stars, received some lavender as a present,
bought patchouli, rose, and paint thinner,
books and stamps and 25-watt bulbs.

It is all here in a cluttered cache,
my luck, my dreams, and privacy. How well
I have seen the temporal fact of it all, but
less every moment do I want to leave it all,
or carry it with me. I ask, not where can I go,

but how can I go, as the shawl and the shelf
grow dearer and I more within, more within?

Kitchen

Flour is exhaustion.
There's always some
in the bag's bottom.

Butter is pain
and in the heat
it can only weep.

Salt is tears,
and cheap.

Onions are the same tunes
to their centers,
always singing to me.
It is their faith
that makes me cry—
they think I'll stop cutting.

Milk is a satisfied whisper.
Oranges
are harmony, one-two,
two-three,
and won't subdue
their shape to the bowl.
The child won't subdue
his shape to the shoe.

And the oven
is vast to the toast,
stingy to the turkey.

Broom is the purr
without the cat.

Candles are clever,
clever, clever—
like the cat stretching up
to the handle of the door.

Bones won't go,
bones won't turn
into a rib cage,
find the leg bones,
and go.

Sweetie pie, why
go out with the ashes?
Cookie, why?

Patchouli

If every man were a clove and ginger
man, all smiles while the storm shook the glass,
if every cookie shaped like a horse
could tempt snow into cedars and paths,
if the candlelight looked down on
a real person made of flour and spice,
there he would be, all plaid and patchouli,
striking her harmless as gratitude,
harmless as a little chipping bird
at heart, that when he comes close, must fly.

She made her saints of bone, each multiple
and dinosaurian, all those fragments
enormous in possibility. The hands
of the scholar fell together in sleep,
spooned soup by daylight, lived and breathed
to die. The moon paused when she looked
its way, a mask on the sky. Light is not
a disguise for darkness, not yet, not
in her mind, not this day, in her present,
while out of a candle breathes his scent.

It is a waste of time, following men,
but what else can you do, if you do not
know the way to trap one? She followed him
out to the snow in her argyles, in that
town that had winter, knowing she was wrong.
But what is a little light in the window?
What is a circle of flour, little mounds
of soda and salt, recipes like prayers
but the old pursuit? He's the gingerbreadman.
You cannot catch him.

The Kiss

The kiss came to her out of nowhere,
pressed into her mind like light,
a steady impression, an initiation
like a bird that straddles a narrow branch.
The kiss came from the book of Genesis,
from the movable type that spread creation,
repetitive and in demand.

Touching her planet like a spacecraft,
a test of character: standing over an iron.
She does the sleeves and the collar
before the body. Part of it scorches.
She irons the pillowcase
and turns to cover a boiling pot.
The iron burns. Steam hisses,

and spray violates the cloth.
The insect blunders in by the window,
tiny and black. She kills it in her palm,
between her hands. He always thought
his heart was there, between her hands,
his small heart like a small seed
just then growing petals like wings.

Ladies and Cattle

Ladies in long dresses and picture hats,
coming to a stream in the orchard,
hold in their gloves the little fruits
they like for they are tart and green.
Like vanity the apples vanish, like cologne.
They look around the orchard, somewhat afraid
of the cattle and their dark brown sight.
The cows may know more than the ladies
why they are here. What do ladies find
in a fine day, rustling along a packed
dirt road, with apples and something to say?

It's a vagabond life.
They dream along the road in the sunshine,
hear something plunge through the brush.
It is Sunday. It is Saturday. It is
fall, summer, spring. Their white dresses
are flags of surrender to the ferns
they gather, having taken off their gloves
and tucked them into their shirtwaist bands.

And suddenly they realize they have
only recently become such ladies;
they remember other times—smothering
their dolls in their carriages with stolen
fruit, stockings, and shoes, tying hair ribbons
to the fences in some cryptic game.
The dresses were shorter and much dirtier.
The crows that looked down upon them and exclaimed

to this day sound exactly the same.
They can sense the height the crows call from,
the sun burns their cheeks and noses, their
ferns and apples grow heavy as they step
uphill. They expect to walk farther—
the sun will turn around and the sky
will be cloudless, like their memories.

The Woman

The woman
is walking through the brambles
where the golden sheep had idled
leaving enough wool to fill spools.
She is singing,
"They did not leave this
behind for me, they did not
leave this for me."
                        "But what was left
we under swords have always been
allotted," sings Ruth in fields,
laying herself down at Boaz's heels.

And they are dreaming of one another,
one in one dream, one in another,
one in the golden field,
one in *The Golden Bough*.

The wives gather
up egg dishes this morning
in the town, the wives
in the country lift the eggs
out of the hollow.
Debutantes carry baskets
into the dewy garden, following
the early gardeners, cutting
roses with their rose shears.

And I went down
to pick an apple, to pick an apple
off of the tree. And the sound
of the apple dropping, apple dropping,

sent up an echo, sent up an echo
of the graveyard, of the orchard
and the truth of the buried,
of the buried as seed.
Oh buried, you'll leave the graveyard,
leave the graveyard
like the apple tree. Reaching
upward, reaching upward
up to me.

In the War with Death

In the war with death
I watch in the night.
I am bitterly sorry.

Hands reach a cold hearth
where the cold air is cold
in the war with death.

With the flowers I carry,
with a blunt voice I say
I am bitterly sorry.

Tears do their best.
Death has no reason.
It is war with death.

I walk. I worry.
I wake in the night
and am bitterly sorry

and stop for breath—
and the end of breath.
In the war with death
I am bitterly sorry.

"I'd Rather Be a Sparrow
than a Snail"

Finding a dead bird in a broken shell.
The title is from "El Condor Pasa,"
English lyric by Paul Simon.

Your origin:
past generations in a boxy cage
from the black London chimney,
from the air all tainted with sewage
filtering from the filthy Thames.
Bright immigrants without language, without
bundles, they brought one talent: need,
and a facile catch at insects
as they went about their flight. Without
the pests, we disdain the sparrow. When
sparrows are scarce, we want them back again.
So arrive, depart, in the heart
of expedient humanity,
which wants its balance.
The rules surround us like your shell.

To give one another charity—
hidebound offerings
of seed in the snow you speckle with
your branchy feet—that is another law,
a found law: sparrow on the halfshell,
a membrane covering the eyes,
a fully formed beak of orderly welcome
to the work it was not born for.
Explain to me. What I ask
is that you teach me the boundary

between shell-charity and flight.
You do not complain. I want to
bury you tonight in the garden.

"Convenience is a synonym for cruelty.
I am a bearable corpse
in the hollow of your hand.
I rest, my cataracts like those
of one old beggar in the gutter
needing pennies to shut the opaque light.
My smell is easy to take,
the whisper of mortality you forget
and wake. As the maggots squirm
through my unborn flesh, I mention Hell."

I Lie Down

I lie down. Petals slowly cover me.
The tree is repeating what it knows,
slowly, thoughtfully, and when I sigh

I lay down my thoughts like a purse
beside me, like a coat around me,
like gloves crossed over my heart;

like a pile of luggage a yard
away, like golden jewelry in the
bank deposit box in another city.

It has been a long trip
for a woman blowing heavy trumpets
over her every signature.

I lie down. I think I will never
stand again, not when my stockings
fuse with the daylight

and refuse any separation.
I do not move. My breath begins now —
arching like a rainbow into the

heart of the sky, it begins. I change;
like a rescued fish set back in its
element, I lie down.

Tenor

She drives the Volvo through light
falling snow to the deserted airfield,
a fallow field of stone
where the army hangar
they use as an auditorium
is like one burr drifting on the ground.
The other women like a crowd of bees
are standing in their winter coats,
jealous, talking.
And she has no part to play in that,
so she folds her arms over her bosom.
In her cellar at home today
she was going over apples, turning out
the bad ones, mourning
the children's growth,
considering their clothes.
And the narrow speaker, his ordinary
way of speaking, has the tenor walk
into his words.

The following day at her place
which is cold as a barn, the children
color, keeping safe inside the lines.
(But the hair mauve, the skin powder blue,
the vest of the comic gosling purple,
decorated by medals.)
He sits on the ottoman by
the picture of a sun-drenched canyon
tasting tomato juice, they all
sip tomato juice from the cellar.
And his dark appearance does not match
the yellow canyon, the red liquid
slipping down his throat to his heart.

He does not need to clear his throat.
I painted
that peace sign
on your garage.
Ten years.
Still there.
Your people
were floundering.

The children look up, their crayons
clenched in their damp fingers.
When mother tells them
about war, she shows them the peace sign.
She shows them the airfield, the deep sky
deepened by a jet, tiny and high.
She remembers the night before, applause
from people who heard people clapping
at The End of a movie,
applause like a crowd of traps snapping shut.

Whale

The oars are silenced.
The silenced oars silence the echoing
darkness and water, unscrew
the lightbulbs of the phosphorescence.

You have shut your eyes to the sureness
of that tactile evening, the whale
like an old thumb-print of presence,
the gray canvas damp at the surface,
dark and enormous with a small, small eye.
The digits at the shovel of the hand
always knew they could not quite place it.

Listen. Echo is twining on stone.
Marginal, intact, virtual, virtuous
coracle. Rainbow arcs into the ear
like old dry beans, like Mother's warning,
like Wrath of Uncle, "What have we here?"

The vine holds on to what comes next, what
happens: though the stone may crumble
in Hellenic ruin; or be parked by the
Empire mile, carved into, dumb, columbine-
fresheted; or stacked up, handled, managed
and bandied by the Old Man of the Wall;
or cobbled into overshoes and sunken
down, hauling bones by the tarsals,
hauling Zoot suit and cigar
and meeting silt exploding
where it must moan many years.

There the stone dreams of a center sun
that blushes on the east at the skyline,
a branch that opens up a flower by blinking,
a flame that rushes to the stove without thinking,
without saying, "I don't know . . ."

There it dreams that echo swims by now,
dreams echo says to the stone,
You will once again see daylight,
there, there. Believe me,
echo only need hear.

"Wind Saves Woman
in Leap from Building"

newspaper article headline

I come at this a stranger
climbing the back fence
to the stone-cold yard of death.
This is the fence where the gray
air the birds call so substantial
by their unrelenting wings
by which they swim through it
will hear of my unbelief in it.

Down below is the stone-cold
patio of death and I let go.

But some unremembered remembrance
said something I did not hear and

the East Wind that brought
my ancestors here and

the South Wind that I leaned on and
it held my coat and

the North Wind Boreas that took note
when my eyes saw snow and

the West Wind Zephyr that had blown
into a cut once on my shin
and healed it

all came as one

and broke that bone against
the building wall and brought
snow stars to my head and tore
that coat, and kept
my name alive, and I learned
that between my will
and the will of the wind,
the will of the wind is stronger.

A Poem about Eggs

for fern, a vegetarian

Seven eggs in a metal pan,
seven lives stopped still to feed me.
Beautiful desert, do not come back
to me. I am following no path.
The water I am drinking
is real to me, so difficult to have,
from what I have been told
and what I have seen. The identical
white eggs are made by prisoners.
Such fine pure work. No woman in a
skirt comes feeding, no child comes
fearfully, comes choring, no plain
old man comes with a bowl of corn.
Their guardian is a box of stone.
Their assurance is electric.
Their nightmare tunnels in to them
like a bank robber after a safe.
Consider his predatory eye
in a farm of easy wire, the frenzy
of yolk and blood, the loss
of creatures and the brilliant run
underneath a cloudy sky where night
surrounds the animal—one fowl
in his belly, one in his teeth—
and all of this encapsuled
in the tiny mind, the inadequate
brain of something that cackles.
We have sat in the crowded halls

wondering exactly like that, at the
phenomenon of cycle, of egg
and chicken, of *Renaissance* we were
to later discover as the best word
we ever ate in our lives. We hear
of the phoenix, of the butterfly.
Everything must be reborn, and we try.

The Similarity

A double word (like Walla Walla or Bora Bora),
when applied by an Amazon native to a plant,
indicates that the plant has medicinal value.
—statement gleaned from Marcus Welby, M.D.

A jungle loves a jungle. The dust
loves dust in those films of the Dust Bowl.
The letter "t"
stands for tango. The partners dance.
The band can watch one another, the horn
with its stops, the drum like a wedding cake
balanced on its gooey side. The man
and the woman in their likeness
cannot take their eyes from their eyes.
They go where they will.

           But in a studio
the window light preys on the faces
of the class of pale children. Their tights,
the narrow shadows of their clothing folds,
their utilitarian hair, conspire to cut out
the heart of the instructor, their likeness
devours her heart. Their day
is a balanced meal, pieces of flesh,
pieces of grain which is a constant
reminder of the fallen tool
lost in the waist-high vegetation,
a reminder of Rust the Corroder,
Rust the Disease of the plant itself.

The cloud is no cold water, though it
comes from cold water. In the double word,
one word is always
the second word,

they are not identical. The teacher
of dancing puts her double heart,
pulsing and scary, bare and separated,
like that, on the floor at her feet,
and questions: which dancer, using
her double legs, her double arms,
her double eyes and ears, resents being
the second row, would like to carry her own
weight, be her own puppet?
Which dancer already has the chance to
roof-leap through the window, to bridge-jump,
to be dead like the others?

Small and large. Choking, soothing,
they have to see tears in the mirror.
They do not know
they will be hurt, for dust loves dust,
and a jungle loves a jungle.

There Was a Woman

There was a woman who wanted an answer.
She stood by the tree up to her knees
in leaves like discarded lunch sacks.
She printed PARADISE in her palm in ink.
She put an egg in her palm, and circled
her fingers around it. She put money
in her mouth because money talks. She put
ice in the breasts of all her dresses.
The ice melted down to nothing and the money
inflated. But the egg was safe in her palm.

Because it was safe, the egg began to lie.
I am an eagle, it said; when the rabbit
runs along the ground I snatch it. I am
thousands of years old, it said. I am a
rooster in my full maturity. My egg,
your egg—let us not quibble—is a memory
I have cracked from already crowing.

The woman put the egg in a vise.
And when it cracked there was nothing but
a letter inside, reading: I am gone.
I hardly hear you over the telephone.
I won't call. I won't mail you a letter.
I am sorry. I am sorry. But I am gone.

After Rain

She rode along on the earth. She sensed
the earth. It made her think no thought
but that the earth had her in its pocket,
a loaf with a spot of salt,
a brick with a bit of sand.

After rain, a moth on the wall
like a lichen.

She thought of strings and threads,
of length of life—that long threads
tangle, never slip through cloth,
and short threads are not enough.

If you rode along facing west,
or walked like a lemming, maybe the night
would never wander off
from the swollen stars like nailheads,
the knothole of a moon.

About the Author

Laura Jensen was born in Tacoma, Washington, in 1948. She received degrees from the University of Washington and the University of Iowa where she attended the Iowa Writers' Workshop. She has been awarded grants from the National Endowment for the Arts and the Washington State Arts Commission. Her poems have been published in five previous collections and in many of the finest literary magazines and anthologies. She has read her poems widely and served as a visiting poet at Oklahoma State University. She currently lives in Tacoma, Washington.